KU-545-668

FONDUE COOKERY

COOKSHOP

FONDUE COOKERY

Cover and inside photography by Dave Jordan

Published on behalf of
The Boots Company plc, Nottingham
by Hamlyn Publishing,
a division of The Hamlyn Publishing Group Ltd,
Bridge House, London Road, Twickenham, Middlesex, England

ISBN 0 600 32553 9

Set in Gill Sans
by Photocomp Ltd, Birmingham

Printed in Italy

Contents

Useful Facts & Figures

Notes on metrication

In this book quantities are given in metric and Imperial measures. Exact conversion from Imperial to metric measures does not usually give very convenient working quantities and so the metric measures have been rounded off into units of 25 grams. The table below shows the recommended equivalents.

Ounces	Approx g to nearest whole figure	Recommended conversion to nearest unit of 25
1	28	25
2	57	50
3	85	75
4	113	100
5	142	150
6	170	175
7	198	200
8	227	225
9	255	250
10	283	275
11	312	300
12	340	350
13	368	375
14	396	400
15	425	425
16 (1 lb)	454	450
17	482	475
18	510	500
19	539	550
20 (1¼ lb)	567	575

Note: When converting quantities over 20 oz first add the appropriate figures in the centre column, then adjust to the nearest unit of 25. As a general guide, 1 kg (1000 g) equals 2·2 lb or about 2 lb 3 oz. This method of conversion gives good results in nearly all cases, although in certain pastry and cake recipes a more accurate conversion is necessary to produce a balanced recipe.

Liquid measures The millilitre has been used in this book and the following table gives a few examples.

Imperial	Approx ml to nearest whole figure	Recommended ml
¼ pint	142	150 ml
½ pint	283	300 ml
¾ pint	425	450 ml
1 pint	567	600 ml
1½ pints	851	900 ml
1¾ pints	992	1000 ml (1 litre)

Spoon measures All spoon measures given in this book are level unless otherwise stated.

Can sizes At present, cans are marked with the exact (usually to the nearest whole number) metric equivalent of the Imperial weight of the contents, so we have followed this practice when giving can sizes.

Oven temperatures

The table below gives recommended equivalents.

	°C	°F	Gas
Very cool	110	225	¼
	120	250	½
Cool	140	275	1
	150	300	2
Moderate	160	325	3
	180	350	4
Moderately hot	190	375	5
	200	400	6
Hot	220	425	7
	230	450	8
Very hot	240	475	9

Note: *When making any of the recipes in this book, only follow one set of measures as they are not interchangeable.*

Introduction

A quick look through the pages of this book will show you that there is an enormous variety of recipes to choose from. There are traditional recipes from Switzerland where fondue is the national dish. There are lots of stories about the origins of the Swiss fondue; one of them tells of villagers who were without food during one very harsh winter so they lived on their own supply of simple produce which consisted of cheese bread and wine. As the cheese hardened and became stale, they melted it in the wine and ate it with the bread.

In addition to simple fondues, the chapters which follow offer a host of new ideas for cheese fondues as well as fish, meat and vegetables. There are sauces and accompaniments with lots of exciting menu suggestions. In addition, there are a few drinks recipes which are particularly suitable for serving to accompany a fondue meal. Should you favour the dessert course of the meal, you will find a chapter on sweet fondues along with suggestions as to how best to introduce them into the menu.

If you decide to serve a simple cheese fondue, then you may find that it turns out to be an inexpensive meal as well as offering a fun way of entertaining. Among the traditions surrounding the serving and eating of fondue are the light hearted ideas of drinking a whole glass of wine or having the honour (or embarrassment) of having to kiss each of the guests should you accidentally drop of piece of food off the fork into the fondue pan. Serving fondue to several guests can be great fun and it is a good idea to make sure you have a couple of spirit burners and pans ready to satisfy hungry appetites. It is always surprising how much people can eat when the form of the meal is as casual and informal as in the case of fondue.

There are just a few points to remember when you prepare a fondue. For cheese fondues you will need a fairly heavy pan — metal, lined with enamel, or one which has a cast iron base to prevent the cheese from burning quickly. The ideal pan to use for a cheese fondue is a heavy, glazed earthenware pot. Bourguignonne fondues or those which require large pots of simmering stock require a metal pan which will transmit heat quickly to keep the cooking liquid at the highest temperature possible. If these thin metal pans are used for a cheese fondue then they will burn quickly and to an undesirable extent.

Lastly, to end a perfect cheese fondue meal, when the pot is wiped clean, the rich, cheese crust which coats the base of the pan is considered to be the delicacy which is shared between all guests.

Cheese Fondues

Here you will find an interesting selection of traditional and exciting new ideas for cheese-based fondues. Flavoured with various additional ingredients, herbs and spices, the recipes offer lots of serving suggestions, and menus are also featured. It is also worth remembering that in addition to offering an excellent way of entertaining informally, many of the recipes in this chapter are quite economical to prepare.

DUTCH FONDUE

SERVES 4

1 clove garlic
150 ml/¼ pint dry white wine
1 teaspoon lemon juice
450 g/1 lb Gouda or Edam cheese, grated
1 tablespoon cornflour
1½ tablespoons brandy
freshly ground black pepper
pinch of ground nutmeg

Rub the inside of a fondue pan with the cut clove of garlic. Pour in the wine and lemon juice and heat gently until almost boiling. Gradually add the cheese, stirring continuously until melted. Blend the cornflour with the brandy and stir into the fondue. Continue to cook over a low heat, stirring until thickened. Add the pepper and nutmeg.

Serving Suggestion
Use cubes of French bread and celery sticks to dip into the fondue.

FARMHOUSE FONDUE

SERVES 4

1 clove garlic
450 g/1 lb Cheddar cheese, grated
150 ml/¼ pint milk
salt and freshly ground black pepper
pinch of dry mustard
pinch of ground nutmeg
2 tablespoons dry white wine (optional)

Rub the inside of a fondue pan with the cut clove of garlic. Add the cheese and melt over a low heat, stirring continuously.

Gradually add the remaining ingredients and cook until thickened and creamy, stirring all the time.

Serving Suggestion
Serve cubes of fried bread, pretzels and bread sticks to dip into the fondue, and accompany with a crisp Green Salad (see page 58).

Note: This is not a stringy fondue.

Dutch Fondue

GUACAMOLE FONDUE
SERVES 4

450 ml/¾ pint dry white wine
450 g/1 lb Emmental cheese, grated
25 g/1 oz flour
1 ripe avocado pear
1 clove garlic, crushed
1 tablespoon lemon juice
150 ml/¼ pint double cream
few drops of Tabasco sauce
freshly ground black pepper

Pour the wine into a fondue pan and heat gently. Toss the cheese and flour together and gradually add to the pan, stirring continuously until melted.

Peel, stone and mash the avocado and stir into the fondue with the remaining ingredients. Reheat, stirring all the time, but *do not allow to boil.*

Serving Suggestion

Serve peeled prawns and cooked scampi to dip into the fondue, and accompany with a Niçoise Salad (see page 55).

CRISPY BACON AND SPINACH FONDUE
SERVES 4

600 ml/1 pint dry cider
450 g/1 lb Lancashire cheese, crumbled
2 tablespoons cornflour
1 (227-g/8-oz) packet
frozen chopped spinach
225 g/8 oz rindless lean bacon, chopped
pinch of ground nutmeg
freshly ground black pepper

Pour the cider into a fondue pan and heat gently. Add the cheese and cornflour gradually, allowing the cheese to melt, and stir continuously.

Cook the spinach according to the packet instructions and drain well. Sauté the bacon in its own fat until crisp. Drain well on kitchen paper.

Stir the cooked spinach into the fondue with the nutmeg and black pepper to taste. Reheat gently and sprinkle the crispy bacon over the top.

Serving Suggestion

Serve with cubes of fried white bread to dip into the fondue.

MENU

Egg and Anchovy Mayonnaise

Lobster Fondue, served with prawns, scallops, smoked salmon and smoked mussels
French Bread
Swiss Rosti

Fresh Fruit Salad and Cream

Egg and Anchovy Mayonnaise
This is a deliciously simple variation on a simple egg mayonnaise. Hard-boil four eggs, shell them and cut in half, then arrange on individual plates. Mash 1 (56-g/2-oz) can of anchovies with their oil and mix into 150 ml/¼ pint thoroughly chilled mayonnaise. Add a dash of lemon juice and freshly ground black pepper to taste. Spoon the anchovy mayonnaise over the eggs, sprinkle with a little paprika and garnish with lemon wedges. Chill lightly before serving.

Swiss Rosti
Fry 100 g/4 oz finely chopped rindless bacon in a large non-stick frying pan. Add 450 g/1 lb grated potatoes, seasoning to taste and a knob of butter. Mix well, then press flat and cook gently until golden underneath. Turn the potato cake out on to a large plate, then slide it back into the pan and cook the second side until golden. Serve immediately.

Fresh Fruit Salad
Make a light syrup using 50 g/2 oz sugar to 150 ml/¼ pint water, set aside to cool. Prepare a selection of fruits according to their type: oranges, apples, strawberries, melon, pears, grapes, kiwi fruit and banana. Pour the syrup over the fruit and chill lightly before serving with cream.

SORREL FONDUE

S E R V E S 4

1 clove garlic
450 ml/¾ pint dry white wine
450 g/1 lb Emmental cheese, grated
2 tablespoons flour
100 g/4 oz fresh sorrel
freshly ground black pepper

Rub the inside of a fondue pan with the cut clove of garlic. Pour in the wine and heat gently. Toss the cheese and flour together lightly, then gradually stir into the wine until the cheese has melted.

Cook the sorrel in boiling, salted water until soft. Drain well and blend in a liquidiser to make a purée. Stir into the fondue with black pepper to taste. Reheat and serve.

Serving Suggestion
Bite-sized chunks of granary bread or wholemeal bread and sticks of celery are good to dip into this fondue.

Note: Sorrel (the whole leaves are shown in the picture above) is a perennial plant native to Europe and Asia. It has a slightly acidic, bitter tang which complements a rich cheese fondue such as this one. However, if you are unable to obtain sorrel, then you may like to substitute cooked spinach or watercress. Both of these ingredients will make interesting additions to the basic fondue.

HAM AND HORSE-RADISH FONDUE
S E R V E S 2

225 g/8 oz mature Cheddar cheese, grated
15 g/½ oz butter
4 tablespoons milk
2 teaspoons grated horseradish
freshly ground black pepper
1 tablespoon flour
2 tablespoons dry white wine or dry sherry
225 g/8 oz cooked ham, finely chopped
½ teaspoon wholegrain mustard

Place the cheese and butter in a fondue pan and allow to melt over a low heat, stirring continuously. Stir in the milk, horseradish and pepper. Blend the flour with the wine until smooth and stir into the fondue. Reheat gently, stirring until the fondue has thickened, then mix in the ham and mustard.

Serving Suggestion
Sticks of celery and celeriac give some crunch to this fondue, together with a Cauliflower Salad (see page 53).

Note: 1 teaspoon creamed horseradish sauce may be used instead of grated horseradish.

Celeriac is a root vegetable which has a similar flavour to celery. The celeriac resembles a swede in size and it has a thick skin. It can be eaten raw or cooked. To serve with fondue, cut the root into thick slices, peel them and cut into small cubes. Wash and toss these in lemon juice to prevent discolouration. If preferred, the celeriac can be cooked in boiling salted water for 2 minutes but it should not be overcooked or its crunchy texture will be lost.

SEAFOOD FONDUE
S E R V E S 4

1 clove garlic
150 ml/¼ pint dry white wine
450 g/1 lb Emmental cheese, grated
1 tablespoon cornflour
1 tablespoon chopped parsley
salt and freshly ground black pepper
1 tablespoon dry sherry
100 g/4 oz peeled prawns
100 g/4 oz frozen cooked mussels, defrosted
225 g/8 oz smoked mackerel, flaked
1 teaspoon lemon juice

Rub the inside of a fondue pan with the cut clove of garlic. Pour in the wine and heat gently. Toss the cheese and cornflour together and gradually add to the pan, stirring continuously until the cheese has melted. Add the parsley, seasoning and sherry and cook until the fondue has thickened.

Stir in the prawns, mussels and mackerel, then add the lemon juice and reheat gently.

Serving Suggestion
Serve with plenty of hot granary bread cut into neat cubes and a Niçoise Salad (see page 55). If you would like to offer a particularly special accompaniment with the fondue, then prepare some scallops, cut them in half and wrap each in a piece of lean streaky bacon. Skewer the wrapped scallops and cook under a hot grill until golden. Serve hot to dip in the fondue.

Note: To prepare fresh scallops, first open the shells with a strong knife and slide it between the scallop and the rounded shell. Rinse the scallop and discard all but the neat, white round of muscle and the bright red coral.

Seafood Fondue

LOBSTER FONDUE
SERVES 4

600 ml/1 pint dry white wine
450 g/1 lb Gruyère cheese, grated
2 tablespoons cornflour
1 (227-g/8-oz) can lobster meat
freshly ground black pepper
paprika to sprinkle

Pour the white wine into a fondue pan and heat gently. Gradually stir in the cheese and cornflour over a low heat, until the cheese has melted.

Drain the lobster meat and divide into bite-sized flakes. Stir into the fondue with black pepper to taste and reheat. Sprinkle with paprika.

Serving Suggestion
For a special occasion serve peeled prawns, poached scallops, small rolls of smoked salmon and smoked mussels to dip into the fondue, and plenty of hot French bread to accompany it.

APPLE CHEESE FONDUE
SERVES 6

450 ml/¾ pint dry apple juice
675 g/1½ lb Gruyère cheese, grated
2 tablespoons flour
2 tablespoons Calvados (apple brandy)
salt and freshly ground black pepper
pinch of ground nutmeg

Pour the apple juice into a fondue pan and heat gently. Toss the cheese and flour together and gradually add to the wine, stirring continuously until melted. Add the remaining ingredients and cook over a low heat until thickened.

Serving Suggestion
Serve with pretzels, frankfurter sausages and plenty of rye bread.

Apple Cheese Fondue

NEUCHÂTEL FONDUE
SERVES 4

1 clove garlic
150 ml/¼ pint dry white wine
1 teaspoon lemon juice
275 g/10 oz Emmental cheese, grated
275 g/10 oz Gruyère cheese, grated
1 tablespoon cornflour
3 tablespoons Kirsch liqueur
pinch of white pepper
pinch of ground nutmeg
pinch of paprika

Rub the inside of a fondue pan with the cut clove of garlic. Pour the wine and lemon juice into the pan and heat gently. Gradually add the cheeses, stirring continuously until melted.

When the fondue begins to bubble, blend the cornflour with the Kirsch and stir in. Cook gently for 2-3 minutes then add the rest of the seasonings.

Serving Suggestion
Cubes of French bread are traditionally served with this fondue, although a selection of fresh salad vegetables, such as spring onions, peppers, radishes, chicory and celeriac, add a contrast of textures.

APPLE AND FRESH HERB FONDUE
SERVES 4

1 clove garlic
150 ml/¼ pint apple juice
450 g/1 lb Gruyère cheese, grated
1 tablespoon cornflour
1 teaspoon chopped parsley
1 teaspoon chopped chives
1 teaspoon chopped thyme
salt and freshly ground black pepper

Rub the inside of a fondue pan with the cut clove of garlic. Pour in the apple juice and heat gently.

Toss the cheese and cornflour together then gradually add to the pan, stirring continuously until melted. Mix in the herbs and seasoning and reheat, stirring until thickened.

Serving Suggestion
A selection of garlic sausage and continental sausage, cut into chunks, is delicious with this fondue, together with hot garlic bread.

MENU

Smoked Mackerel Pâté

Crispy Bacon Fondue
Cubes of Crusty Bread
Aubergine Salad

Oranges in Caramel Sauce

Smoked Mackerel Pâté
Remove skin from 225 g/8 oz smoked mackerel. Blend in a food processor or liquidiser, together with 2-3 tablespoons lemon juice, 100 g/4 oz melted butter and 1 tablespoon creamed horseradish. Lightly whisk 150 ml/¼ pint double cream and fold it into the fish until evenly mixed. Season to taste. Chill and serve with wedges of lemon and melba toast.

Oranges in Caramel Sauce
Peel 6 oranges, removing all the pith, and cut the flesh into slices. Place in an ovenproof dish and sprinkle with 3 tablespoons Cointreau. Place 225 g/ 8 oz granulated sugar and 300 ml/½ pint water in a saucepan and dissolve over a low heat. When the sugar has completely dissolved bring to the boil and cook until the syrup turns to a light caramel. Pour the caramel over the oranges immediately and leave overnight if possible, so that the caramel becomes syrupy. Sprinkle with chopped pistachio nuts and serve with clotted cream.

ONION AND CARAWAY FONDUE
S E R V E S 4 - 6

50 g/2 oz butter
225 g/8 oz onions, chopped
2 teaspoons caraway seeds
300 ml/½ pint dry white wine
350 g/12 oz Gruyère cheese, grated
350 g/12 oz Emmental cheese, grated
1 teaspoon wholegrain mustard
pinch of ground nutmeg
1 tablespoon cornflour
2 tablespoons vermouth

Melt the butter in a fondue pan and sauté the onion and caraway seeds for 5-10 minutes, until soft but not browned. Pour in the wine and heat gently. Gradually add the cheeses, stirring continuously until melted. Add the mustard and nutmeg.

Blend the cornflour with the vermouth and stir into the fondue. Cook over a low heat until thickened, stirring continuously.

Serving Suggestion
Serve with baked jacket potatoes, frankfurter sausages, salami and a bowl of Sauerkraut Salad (see page 53).

Note: If you find the flavour of caraway seeds too strong, then try using fennel seeds or lightly toasted sesame seeds in the above recipe.

GRUYÈRE FONDUE WITH WALNUTS
S E R V E S 3 - 4

1 clove garlic
450 ml/¾ pint dry white wine
350 g/12 oz Gruyère cheese, grated
2 tablespoons cornflour
25 g/1 oz butter
2 tablespoons brandy
pinch of ground nutmeg
freshly ground black pepper
75 g/3 oz walnuts, finely chopped

Place the garlic and wine in a saucepan, bring to the boil and reduce the liquor by fast boiling to about 350 ml/ 12 fl oz. Remove the garlic and pour the liquor into a

Onion and Caraway Fondue

fondue pan.

Toss the cheese and cornflour together and gradually add to the pan, stirring continuously until melted. Stir in the butter and allow to melt. Add the remaining ingredients and reheat gently.

Serving Suggestion
Serve with cubes of ham to dip into the fondue and accompany with a bowl of Sauerkraut Salad (see page 53).

TUNA AND FRESH TOMATO FONDUE
S E R V E S 4

50 g/2 oz butter
1 (198-g/7-oz) can tuna fish in oil
2 onions, finely chopped
225 g/8 oz mature Cheddar cheese, grated
2 tablespoons dry sherry
450 g/1 lb tomatoes, skinned,
deseeded and chopped
2 tablespoons chopped fresh basil
or 1 teaspoon dried basil

Place the butter in a fondue pan with the drained oil from the tuna fish. Add and sauté the chopped onion until softened but not browned.

Gradually add the cheese and sherry, stirring continuously over a low heat until the fondue is smooth and creamy. Separate the tuna fish into chunks and add with the remaining ingredients. Heat the fondue carefully, taking care not to break down the fish too much.

Serving Suggestion
Serve with chunks of peeled cucumber, pickled onions and French bread.

Note: To skin tomatoes, place the fruit in a bowl and pour on enough freshly boiling water to cover the tomatoes completely. Leave for 30-60 seconds depending on the ripeness of the fruit. Drain and use a sharp pointed knife to slit the skin which can then be peeled away easily.

CURRIED CHEESE FONDUE

SERVES 4-6

1 clove garlic
300 ml/½ pint dry white wine
450 g/1 lb Gruyère cheese, grated
225 g/8 oz Emmental cheese, grated
2 teaspoons cornflour
1 teaspoon curry paste
1 tablespoon water
salt and freshly ground black pepper
1 teaspoon lemon juice

Rub the inside of a fondue pan with the cut clove of garlic. Pour in the wine and heat gently. Gradually add the cheeses, stirring continuously until melted.

Blend the cornflour and curry paste together with the water and stir into the fondue. Continue to cook over a gentle heat, stirring all the time until thickened. Add the seasoning and lemon juice.

Serving Suggestion

Serve with chunks of cucumber, poppadums and Naan bread (available in the form of a packet mix). A bowl of Tomato Salad (see page 62) will complement the richness of this fondue.

Note: If preferred, you can grind your own curry spices to use instead of the bought curry paste in the above recipe. Take 1 tablespoon cumin seeds, 2 tablespoons coriander seeds and the small black seeds scraped from inside 3 green cardamon pods. Put these spices in a small, heavy-based pan with 1 cinnamon stick and cook gently, stirring frequently until the seeds are evenly and lightly toasted. Allow to cool slightly, then grind the spices to a fine powder and add a pinch of chilli powder, ½ teaspoon turmeric and enough water to make a smooth paste.

MENU

Leeks Vinaigrette

Gruyère Fondue with Walnuts
French Bread
Sauerkraut

French Apple Flan and Cream

Leeks Vinaigrette

Trim and wash 4-8 leeks and cook them in lightly salted boiling water until just tender – about 5 minutes. Drain and transfer to a serving dish. In a screw-topped jar, shake together 6 tablespoons olive oil, 2 tablespoons wine vinegar, 1 crushed clove garlic, ½ teaspoon caster sugar and seasoning to taste. Pour over the hot leeks and sprinkle with plenty of chopped parsley. Chill lightly before serving.

French Apple Flan

Make shortcrust pastry using 225 g/8 oz plain flour and 175 g/6 oz butter (or buy frozen pastry). Roll out to line a 20-cm/8-in flan dish and prick the base all over with a fork. Bake blind in a moderately hot oven (190 C, 375 F, gas 5) for 15 minutes. Peel, core and slice 450 g/1 lb cooking apples and arrange them in the flan case. Sprinkle with a little lemon juice and 2 tablespoons caster sugar. Bake for 30 minutes, or until the apples are tender. Warm and sieve 225 g/8 oz apricot jam and use to glaze the apples. Serve warm with cream.

STILTON FONDUE

SERVES 4

450 ml/¾ pint lager
75 g/3 oz Stilton cheese
350 g/12 oz mild Cheddar cheese, grated
1 tablespoon flour
freshly ground black pepper

Pour the lager into a fondue pan and heat gently. Crumble the Stilton as finely as possible and gradually stir into the lager until completely melted. Toss the Cheddar cheese and flour together and add gradually, stirring all the time until the cheese has melted and the fondue thickened. Season with black pepper.

Serving Suggestion
Serve with a selection of vegetables such as crisp celery sticks, canned baby sweet corn and water chestnuts.

Beer Fondue

BEER FONDUE

SERVES 6

750 ml/1 ¼ pints pale ale
675 g/1 ½ lb Cheshire cheese, grated
few drops of Tabasco sauce
2 teaspoons Worcestershire sauce
pinch of dry mustard
freshly ground black pepper
2 tablespoons cornflour

Heat the beer in a fondue pan, add the cheese and heat gently until it has melted. Stir in the Tabasco, Worcestershire sauce, mustard and seasoning. Blend the cornflour with a little cold water and stir into the fondue. Heat, stirring all the time until thickened.

Serving Suggestion
Serve with cubes of bread to dip into the fondue, a bowl of pickled onions, gherkins, baked jacket potatoes and an Orange Coleslaw (see page 61).

THREE-CHEESE FONDUE

SERVES 6

1 clove garlic
50 g/2 oz butter
1-2 sticks celery, finely chopped
300 ml/½ pint dry white wine
350 g/12 oz Emmental cheese, grated
350 g/12 oz Gruyère cheese, grated
50 g/2 oz Parmesan cheese, grated
pinch of dry mustard
pinch of ground nutmeg
pinch of cayenne
1 tablespoon cornflour
2 tablespoons brandy

Rub the inside of a fondue pan with the cut clove of garlic. Melt the butter and sauté the celery for 5-10 minutes.

Stir in the wine and heat gently. Gradually add the cheeses, stirring continuously until melted. Season with mustard, nutmeg and cayenne. Blend the cornflour with the brandy and stir into the fondue. Gradually bring to the boil and cook over a *low* heat for 5-10 minutes, stirring all the time.

Serving Suggestion
Serve with cubes of French bread and peeled shrimps to dip into the fondue.

Note: Prepared fondues can be frozen quite successfully. If you have any fondue left after a meal, or if you want to prepare the meal well in advance. Make sure the fondue is smooth and thoroughly combined, then allow it to cool slightly (but not long enough to become firm). Pour the fondue into a freezer container and it will keep for up to 6 months. To reheat, transfer the defrosted fondue to a heavy pan and heat gently, stirring continuously.

CREAMED ASPARAGUS FONDUE

SERVES 4 - 6

150 ml/¼ pint dry cider
450 g/1 lb Emmental cheese, grated
1 tablespoon flour
1 (298-g/10½-oz) can condensed
asparagus soup
freshly ground black pepper
pinch of cayenne
3 tablespoons dry sherry

Pour the cider into a fondue pan and heat gently. Toss the cheese and flour together and gradually add to the cider, stirring continuously until melted.

Stir in the soup and cook over a low heat until the fondue has thickened. Add the remaining ingredients and reheat.

Serving Suggestion
Serve with celery sticks, cubes of peeled cucumber and granary bread.

Note: To make a very special, fresh asparagus fondue substitute 450 g/1 lb fresh asparagus for the condensed soup in the above recipe. Trim the asparagus and cook it in boiling salted water for about 20 minutes or until tender. Ideally the vegetable should be tied in a neat bundle and stood upright in a tall, lidded saucepan so that the tender tips cook in the steam rather than the water. Drain and chop the cooked asparagus and stir it into the fondue instead of the soup.

Three-Cheese Fondue

MUSHROOM AND MUSTARD FONDUE
SERVES 3 - 4

*350 g/12 oz small button mushrooms,
trimmed and cleaned
50 g/2 oz butter
1 teaspoon oil
3 tablespoons flour
250 ml/8 fl oz milk
100 g/4 oz Emmental cheese, grated
1-2 teaspoons wholegrain mustard
150 ml/¼ pint double cream
salt and freshly ground black pepper*

To ensure that the fondue does not turn dark grey in colour, it is best to use the closed, pale mushrooms. Chop them evenly and finely.

Put the butter and oil in a fondue pan and heat until the butter melts. Add and gently sauté the mushrooms for 5-10 minutes stirring frequently, stir in the flour, then gradually pour in the milk and bring to the boil, stirring all the time. Cook for 1 minute.

Reduce the heat and stir in the cheese then continue to cook over a low heat, until the cheese has melted. Add the remaining ingredients, stirring continuously. Reheat, but *do not allow to boil.*

Serving Suggestion
Serve with cubes or slices of French bread fried in butter flavoured with a pinch of curry powder and crisp, grilled bacon rolls.

Note: There is a wide variety of different mustards to choose from. Wholegrain mustard can be mild or strong, flavoured with herbs, honey or spices. Other types of mustard are available in different strengths, mixed with horseradish, sage and onion or chives. If you are particularly keen on mustard, then increase the amount which you add to the fondue; for a robust result use 2-3 tablespoons of the chosen mustard.

CHEESE AND PINEAPPLE FONDUE
S E R V E S 4

150 ml/¼ pint dry white wine
225 g/8 oz Emmental or
Gruÿère cheese, grated
225 g/8 oz mature Cheddar cheese, grated
1 teaspoon cornflour
1 teaspoon caster sugar
1 tablespoon Kirsch liqueur
½ teaspoon wholegrain mustard
freshly ground black pepper
1 (376-g/13¼-oz) can crushed pineapple,
drained

Pour the wine into a fondue pan and heat gently. Toss the cheeses and cornflour together and gradually add to the pan, stirring continuously until melted. Add the sugar, Kirsch, mustard, pepper and crushed pineapple and reheat gently, stirring all the time, but do not allow to boil.

Serving Suggestion
Serve with a platter of crudités, such as sticks of raw carrot, celery and celeriac, strips of pepper, cauliflower florets and radishes. Have plenty of hot French bread and a Green Salad (see page 58) to accompany the fondue.

Note: Fresh pineapple can be used in the above recipe. Select a small ripe fruit; cut off the ends and remove the peel, then cut out all the eyes. Halve the pineapple and remove the core, then finely chop the fruit. Alternatively, cut the pineapple into chunks and put it through a food processor or liquidiser.

MENU

Fresh Tomato Soup with Basil

Cheese and Pineapple Fondue
Crudités
French Bread
Green Salad

Meringues with Strawberries

Fresh Tomato Soup with Basil
Wash 675 g/1½ lb tomatoes and cut into quarters. Finely slice 1 onion and 1 carrot and sauté these in 25 g/1 oz butter until soft. Remove from the heat and stir in 25 g/1 oz plain flour. Add the tomatoes, 600 ml/1 pint chicken stock, a bay leaf, a pinch each of sugar and mace, 2 teaspoons freshly chopped basil and seasoning to taste. Bring to the boil and simmer for 20-30 minutes. Blend in a food processor or liquidiser, then sieve to remove the tomato skins. Reheat and serve with a little cream, if liked

Crudités
Prepare a selection of raw ingredients to dip in the fondue. For example small florets of cauliflower, neat sticks of celery and carrot, scrubbed radishes, cubes of celeriac and wedges of apple, both dipped in lemon juice.

Meringues with Strawberries
Whisk 2 egg whites until very stiff, then add 100 g/ 4 oz caster sugar a little at a time, whisking until stiff. Pipe or spoon the meringue in small mounds onto baking sheets lined with non-stick paper. Bake in a very cool oven (110 C, 225 F, gas ¼) for 2-3 hours. Remove and cool on a wire tray. Serve with fresh strawberries and cream.

SWEET CORN AND PEPPER FONDUE

SERVES 4

1 red pepper
1 green pepper
25 g/1 oz butter
150 ml/¼ pint dry cider
450 g/1 lb Gruyère cheese, grated
2 teaspoons cornflour
1 (340-g/12-oz) can creamed sweet corn
2 tablespoons chopped parsley
salt and freshly ground black pepper

Cut the stalk ends off the peppers. Remove the seeds and chop the pepper shells, then fry these in the butter in the fondue pan until soft but not browned.

Pour the cider into the fondue pan and heat gently. Toss the cheese and cornflour together and gradually add to the pan, stirring continuously until melted.

Add the sweet corn and stir into the fondue with the remaining ingredients. Cook over a low heat until thickened, stirring continuously.

Serving Suggestion

Serve cooked cocktail sausages and plenty of hot granary bread or white bread cut into cubes to dip into the fondue.

Note: Finely chopped black olives and spring onions can be stirred into the fondue with the sweet corn.

DEVILLED CRAB FONDUE
S E R V E S   4

150 ml/¼ pint dry white wine
450 g/1 lb Gruyère cheese, grated
1 tablespoon cornflour
1 (169-g/6-oz) can crabmeat, flaked
1 teaspoon Worcestershire sauce
½ teaspoon wholegrain mustard
freshly ground black pepper
few drops of Tabasco sauce

Pour the wine into a fondue pan and heat gently. Toss the cheese and cornflour together and gradually add to the pan, stirring continuously until melted. Add the crabmeat and remaining ingredients. Reheat, stirring.

Serving Suggestion
Serve with cubes of bread, fried in garlic butter and accompany with a Tomato Salad (see page 62).

MENU

Hot Herb Bread

Smoky Bacon Fondue
Cubes of Pineapple
French Bread
Celery Sticks

Ice Cream with Chocolate Sauce

Hot Herb Bread
Beat 4 tablespoons chopped fresh herbs into 100 g/ 4 oz butter. Cut a French loaf almost through into slices, leaving the pieces attached at the base. Spread the herb butter between the slices, wrap in foil and bake in a moderately hot oven (200 C, 400 F, gas 6) for 15-20 minutes.

Ice Cream with Chocolate Sauce
Serve good-quality, bought ice cream. Melt 225 g/ 8 oz plain chocolate with 4 tablespoons golden syrup and 25 g/1 oz butter in a basin over a saucepan of hot water. Stir well, then serve with the ice cream.

SMOKY BACON FONDUE
S E R V E S   4

150 ml/¼ pint dry white wine
450 g/1 lb Gruyère cheese, grated
1 tablespoon cornflour
225 g/8 oz rindless lean smoked bacon
1 teaspoon chopped parsley
freshly ground black pepper
pinch of paprika

Pour the wine into a fondue pan and heat gently. Toss the cheese and cornflour together and gradually add to the pan, stirring continuously until melted.

Chop the bacon finely and fry in its own fat until crisp. Drain well on kitchen paper. Add to the fondue with the remaining ingredients and cook over a low heat until thickened.

Serving Suggestion
Serve with cubes of fresh pineapple, celery sticks and French bread.

Smoky Bacon Fondue

Sage Fondue

SAGE FONDUE
SERVES 4

1 clove garlic
450 ml/¾ pint dry white wine
450 g/1 lb Gruyère cheese, grated
75 g/3 oz Sage Derby cheese, grated
25 g/1 oz flour
2 tablespoons chopped fresh sage or
1 teaspoon dried sage
freshly ground black pepper

Rub the inside of a fondue pan with the cut clove of garlic. Pour in the wine and heat gently. Toss the cheeses and flour together then gradually add to the pan, stirring continuously until melted. Stir in the sage and black pepper and reheat until thickened.

Serving Suggestion
Serve with a selection of bread sticks, warm croissants, celery sticks, sticks of courgette, cauliflower florets and French bread.

LYMESWOLD FONDUE
SERVES 4

450 ml/¾ pint dry white wine
350 g/12 oz Emmental cheese, grated
100 g/4 oz Lymeswold cheese, crumbled
25 g/1 oz flour
4 tablespoons dry cider
pinch of ground nutmeg
freshly ground black pepper

Pour the wine into the fondue pan and heat gently. Toss the cheeses and flour together then gradually add to the pan, stirring continuously until melted. Cook until the fondue has thickened, then stir in the remaining ingredients.

Serving Suggestion
Chunks of crisp dessert apple go particularly well with this fondue, accompanied by a Green Salad (see page 58).

Fish, Meat & Vegetable Fondues

One of the most appealing characteristics of the fondues in this chapter is that they involve each person in cooking their own food at the dining table. The recipes range from the well-known Fondue Bourguignonne to an interesting Oriental Fondue. Fish, vegetable and chicken fondues are included as well as meat recipes. The sauces and relishes which accompany these fondues play an important part in ensuring their success, so plenty of ideas are proffered.

FRANKFURTER BEEF FONDUE

SERVES 4

1 red pepper
1 green pepper
675 g/1½ lb lean rump steak
450 g/1 lb cocktail frankfurter sausages
oil for cooking
Sweet corn relish:
1 (275-g/10-oz) can creamed sweet corn
2 teaspoons made English mustard
salt and freshly ground black pepper
Cucumber relish:
1 small cucumber, trimmed and finely chopped
1 small onion, finely chopped
1 tablespoon oil
1 teaspoon wholegrain mustard
1 teaspoon cornflour
2 tablespoons vinegar

Cut the ends off the peppers, remove the seeds, then reserve about a quarter of each for the relishes. Cut the rest into chunks. Cut the meat into cubes. Finely chop the reserved pieces of pepper.

Mix the ingredients for the sweet corn relish, adding half the reserved chopped peppers. Fry the cucumber and onion for the cucumber relish in the oil in a small saucepan until soft but not brown. Add the mustard. Blend the cornflour with the vinegar, add to the pan and bring to the boil. Simmer for 3 minutes, then transfer to a serving dish.

Half-fill a fondue pan with oil and heat. Test the temperature as for Fondue Bourguignonne (see page 41) and keep the oil hot over a spirit burner on the table.

Each person spears pieces of steak, frankfurter and pepper, then cooks the food to taste in the oil. The cooked food is eaten with the relishes.

Serving Suggestion
Serve with baked potatoes, Green Salad (see page 58) and Orange Coleslaw (see page 61).

Frankfurter Beef Fondue

VEGETABLE FONDUE

SERVES 4

Select from the following:
cauliflower
small new potatoes
celeriac
okra
courgettes
aubergines
canned artichoke hearts
mushrooms
Batter:
100 g/4 oz plain flour
½ teaspoon salt
1 tablespoon oil
150 ml/¼ pint water
2 egg whites
cooking oil

Prepare the chosen vegetables and cut into bite-sized pieces. If you are using cauliflower, new potatoes, celeriac or okra these should be par-boiled first. Make sure that all the vegetables are thoroughly dry and free from any moisture.

Mix the flour and salt with the oil and water and beat until smooth. Just before you require the batter, whisk the egg whites until stiff and fold into the batter.

Half-fill the fondue pan with cooking oil and heat. Test the temperature as for Fondue Bourguignonne (see page 41) and keep the oil hot over a spirit burner on the table. Spear the chosen vegetable onto a long fondue fork and dip into the batter, making sure it is completely coated. Cook in the hot oil until the batter is crisp and golden.

Serving Suggestion
Serve with Garlic Mayonnaise (see page 48), Guacamole (see page 43) and Provençal Sauce (see page 45), and accompany with a Green Salad (see page 58) and plenty of hot French bread.

CRISPY FISHBALL FONDUE

SERVES 3

50 g/2 oz butter
50 g/2oz flour
150 ml/¼ pint milk
350 g/12 oz smoked cod, cooked
salt and freshly ground black pepper
2 hard-boiled eggs, chopped
1 teaspoon anchovy essence
2 tablespoons chopped parsley
cooking oil
Coating:
beaten egg
fresh white breadcrumbs

Melt the butter in a saucepan and add the flour. Cook over a low heat for 1 minute, stirring all the time. Gradually stir in the milk and bring to the boil. Simmer gently for 1 minute.

Flake the fish and add to the sauce with the remaining ingredients. Spread the mixture over a plate and divide into 12 portions. Chill until firm.

Using floured hands, roll into 12 balls. Dip each in the beaten egg and coat in breadcrumbs.

Pour sufficient oil to come halfway up the fondue pan and heat gently. Test the temperature as for Fondue Bourguignonne (see page 41) and keep the oil hot over a spirit burner on the table. Spear the fishballs and cook in the hot oil.

Serving Suggestion

These fishballs are delicious served with Provençal Sauce (see page 45) and a Chinese Salad (see page 54).

MIXED FISH FONDUE

SERVES 4

225 g/8 oz smoked cod fillet
225 g/8 oz plaice fillets
225 g/8 oz monk fish
cooking oil
Coating:
2 egg whites
1 tablespoon flour
salt and freshly ground black pepper
few drops of Tabasco sauce

Skin the fish and cut into bite-sized pieces, dry thoroughly on kitchen paper.

Lightly whisk the egg whites and mix with the remaining coating ingredients until smooth.

Half-fill the fondue pan with cooking oil and heat. Test the temperature as for Fondue Bourguignonne (see page 41) and keep the oil hot over a spirit burner on the table. Secure a piece of fish on a long fondue fork and dip into the coating. Cook in the hot oil until crisp and golden.

Serving Suggestion
Serve with a Tartare Sauce (see page 48) and Soured Cream Sauce (see page 48), and accompany with an Artichoke and Bean Vinaigrette (see page 57) and baked jacket potatoes.

MENU

Melon and Grapefruit Cocktail

Crispy Fishball Fondue
Provençal Sauce
Chinese Salad
Sautéed Garlic Potatoes

Chocolate Mousse

Melon and Grapefruit Cocktail
Halve a honeydew melon, remove the seeds and scoop out the flesh (use a melon baller). Cut all the peel and pith from 2 grapefruit, then remove each segment of fruit; do this over a bowl to catch all the juice. Mix both fruits with any juice and sprinkle with a little caster sugar to taste. Add a couple of sprigs of fresh mint and chill thoroughly. Serve spooned into individual glass dishes.

Sautéed Garlic Potatoes
Par-boil 450 g/1 lb potatoes, then cut them into thick slices. Melt a knob of butter with 2-3 tablespoons oil in a large frying pan. Add 1 crushed clove garlic, stir, then add the potatoes and fry, turning occasionally, until golden all over. Sprinkle with a little chopped parsley and serve.

Chocolate Mousse
Melt 225 g/8 oz plain chocolate with 50 g/2 oz butter in a basin over hot water. Stir in 2 tablespoons brandy and 2 egg yolks. Cool until just beginning to thicken. Stiffly whisk 2 egg whites, then fold them into the chocolate mixture. Transfer to small individual dishes and chill until set. Serve with single cream.

SMOKED HADDOCK FONDUE

SERVES 4

675 g/1½ lb smoked haddock fillet
1 small onion, chopped
1 carrot, sliced
bouquet garni
few peppercorns
few sprigs of parsley
salt and freshly ground black pepper
300 ml/½ pint white wine

Skin the fish and cut into cubes. Place the trimmings in a saucepan with the remaining ingredients, except the wine. Cover with cold water and boil; simmer for 30 minutes. Strain, season and add the wine. Pour into the fondue pan and bring to the boil. Spear a portion of the fish onto a fondue fork and cook in the boiling fish stock.

Serving Suggestion

Serve with Green Mayonnaise (see page 48), Tartare Sauce (see page 48) and pitta bread stuffed with salad.

CRISPY SCAMPI FONDUE

SERVES 2

1 (284-g/10-oz) packet frozen
Golden Scampi
cooking oil

Place the scampi on individual plates. Pour sufficient oil to come halfway up the fondue pan and heat gently. Test the temperature as for Fondue Bourguignonne (see page 41) and keep the oil hot over a spirit burner on the table.

Spear a portion of scampi onto a fondue fork and cook in the hot oil until golden.

Serving Suggestion

Serve with Tartare Sauce (see page 48), Barbecue Sauce (see page 46) and an Orange Coleslaw (see page 61).

Smoked Haddock Fondue

MARSALA LAMB FONDUE

SERVES 4

675 g/1½ lb fillet of lamb
cooking oil
Marinade:
6 tablespoons Marsala wine
3 tablespoons walnut oil
1 onion, sliced
1 teaspoon turmeric
1 teaspoon ground coriander
1 teaspoon ground cardamom
pinch of cumin seeds
1 tablespoon lemon juice

Cut the lamb into bite-sized pieces. Mix all the marinade ingredients together and marinate the lamb overnight. Drain and dry thoroughly on kitchen paper.

Half-fill a fondue pan with cooking oil and heat. Test the temperature as for Fondue Bourguignonne (see page 41) and keep the oil hot over a spirit burner on the table. Spear a piece of meat onto a fondue fork and cook in the hot oil.

Serving Suggestion

Serve with Cumberland Sauce (see page 44) and Garlic Mayonnaise (see page 48), and accompany with a Pasta Salad (see page 57) and hot French bread.

ROSEMARY LAMB FONDUE

SERVES 4

675 g/1½ lb fillet of lamb
cooking oil
Marinade:
1 clove garlic, crushed
150 ml/¼ pint red wine
2 tablespoons chopped fresh rosemary
1 tablespoon redcurrant jelly
3 tablespoons oil

Cut the lamb into small cubes. Mix all the marinade ingredients and pour into a basin. Add the lamb and mix thoroughly, then cover and leave to marinate overnight in the refrigerator. Drain and dry on absorbent kitchen paper; if the meat is wet it will cause the oil to spit when cooking.

Heat the oil in a fondue pan over a gentle heat as for Fondue Bourguignonne (see page 41). Keep the oil hot over a spirit burner on the table. Serve each person with a portion of the lamb and cook as for Fondue Bourguignonne.

Note: If you like, the marinade can be heated, thickened with cornflour and served with the fondue.

Serving Suggestion

Serve with a Cumberland Sauce (see page 44), a Soured Cream Sauce (see page 48) and Chilled Ratatouille (see page 55).

PORK SATAY FONDUE

SERVES 4

675 g/1½ lb lean pork fillet
cooking oil
Marinade:
300 ml/½ pint coconut milk
2 slices fresh root ginger
1 teaspoon ground coriander
1 teaspoon turmeric
salt and freshly ground black pepper
1 teaspoon dark soft brown sugar

Cut the meat into bite-sized pieces. Mix all the marinade ingredients together and marinate the meat overnight. Drain and dry on kitchen paper.

Pour sufficient oil to come halfway up the fondue pan and heat gently. Test the temperature as for Fondue Bourguignonne (see page 41) and keep the oil hot over a spirit burner on the table.

Serve each person with a portion of the meat. A piece of meat is then speared onto a fondue fork and placed in the hot oil until cooked.

Serving Suggestion

Serve with Satay Sauce (see page 50) and Spiced Rice Salad (see page 63).

ORIENTAL FONDUE
S E R V E S 4

veal fillet
lean pork fillet
chicken breast
calf's liver
1·4 litres/2½ pints chicken stock
3 tablespoons sherry
pinch of dried Provençal herbs

Choose a selection of meats, allowing 150-175 g/5-6 oz per person. Cut the meat into very thin slices and place in individual dishes.

Heat the chicken stock, sherry and herbs in a fire kettle or fondue pan and bring to the boil. Spear a slice of meat onto a fondue fork and cook in the chicken stock. The stock must be kept at boiling point throughout the meal.

Serving Suggestion
Serve with Garlic Mayonnaise (see page 48), Horse-radish Cream Sauce (see page 45) and Madeira Sauce (see page 47), and accompany with a Chinese Salad (see page 54).

Note: The Oriental fondue is totally different from Swiss-style cheese fondues but resembles bourguig-nonne fondues in principle. The pots in which Oriental fondues are traditionally cooked are known as fire pots or chrysanthemum pots. The fire pot is made of a ring-shaped pot which rests on a base in which charcoal burns to provide heat. A central funnel carries away the smoke and serves to heat the pot. A chrysanthemum pot has a pot resting on a spirit burner. The base of the pot has a decorative pattern through which the flames from the burner create a colourful pattern, hence the name chrysanthemum pot. Western fondue pans and burners can be substituted.

MEATBALL FONDUE
S E R V E S 4

1 onion, finely chopped
1 tablespoon oil
450 g/1 lb lean minced beef
pinch of dried thyme
2 tablespoons chopped parsley
salt and freshly ground black pepper
1 egg, beaten
cooking oil

Sauté the onion in the hot oil until soft but not browned. Combine with the remaining ingredients. Using floured hands, shape the mixture into small balls about the size of a walnut.

Pour sufficient oil to come halfway up the fondue pan and heat gently. Test the temperature as for Fondue Bourguignonne (see page 41) and keep the oil hot over a spirit burner on the table. Spear a meatball on the end of a fondue fork and cook in the hot oil.

Serving Suggestion
Serve with Horseradish Cream Sauce (see page 45), Sweet 'n' Sour Sauce (see page 44) and Raita (see page 43), and accompany with a Chinese Salad (see page 54) or an Artichoke and Bean Vinaigrette (see page 57).

Variations
Curried Meatballs Omit the thyme, and add ½ teaspoon curry paste, a pinch of ground cumin, a pinch of ground coriander and ¼ teaspoon ground ginger.
Peanut Meatballs Omit the thyme and add 50 g/ 2 oz finely chopped peanuts and 1 tablespoon peanut butter.
Chilli Meatballs To the basic recipe add 2 table-spoons chilli powder and ½ teaspoon cumin seeds.

MARINATED PORK IN ORANGE FONDUE

SERVES 4

675 g/1 ½ lb lean pork fillet
cooking oil
Marinade:
grated rind and juice of 1 orange
1 clove garlic, crushed
150 ml/¼ pint apple juice
2 tablespoons oil
1 teaspoon soft brown sugar
1 teaspoon cornflour
1 tablespoon water
salt and freshly ground black pepper

Cut the meat into bite-sized pieces. Mix all the marinade ingredients together and marinate the meat overnight. Drain, reserving the marinade, and dry on kitchen paper.

Pour the marinade into a saucepan and bring to the boil. Blend the cornflour with the water, stir into the sauce and simmer for 2 minutes. Add seasoning to taste.

Pour sufficient oil to come halfway up the fondue pan and heat gently. Test the temperature as for Fondue Bourguignonne (see page 41) and keep the oil hot over a spirit burner on the table.

Serve each person with a portion of meat. Spear a piece of meat onto a fondue fork and cook in the hot oil. Serve the hot marinade sauce with the fondue.

Serving Suggestion
Serve with Soured Blue Cheese Dressing (see page 47) and Sweet 'n' Sour Sauce (see page 44) and accompany with sautéed garlic potatoes and a Haricot Salad (see page 61).

FONDUE BOURGUIGNONNE

SERVES 4

*675 g/1 ½ lb fillet or rump steak
cooking oil*

Cut the steak into small cubes. Pour sufficient oil to come halfway up the fondue pan and heat gently. To test the correct temperature of the oil drop in a small piece of bread. If it turns golden brown, the oil is ready for use. Keep the oil hot over a spirit burner on the table, it will cool as more food is cooked and, if necessary, it may need reheating on the hob.

Serve each person with a portion of the meat. A cube of meat is then speared onto the fondue fork and placed in the hot oil, until cooked to the individual's liking.

Serving Suggestion
A selection of sauces such as Raita (see page 43), Green Pepper and Gherkin Sauce (see page 46) and a Chinese Sauce (see page 50) can be served with the meat. You may also like to offer a selection of bought chutneys, mustard and horseradish sauce.

A platter of salad vegetables such as celery, radishes, onion rings and cucumber provide colour and give texture to the fondue. Offer an oil and vinegar dressing with the salad ingredients. Serve with plenty of hot French bread.

Sauces, Dips & Relishes

When you plan a fondue meal it is often essential that you include a selection of sauces which will bring out to the full the flavour of the main ingredients. Throughout the recipes in this book you will find suggestions have been made as to the most suitable accompaniments for the fondues; you may like to follow these or make your own favourite sauces instead. Alternatively, you may feel inspired to try some of the ideas included in this chapter.

GUACAMOLE

2 avocado pears
½ small onion, grated
2 cloves garlic, crushed
1 tablespoon lemon juice
1 tablespoon olive oil
salt and freshly ground black pepper
150 ml/¼ pint soured cream
pinch of cayenne
few drops of Tabasco sauce
watercress sprigs to garnish

Cut the avocado pears in half, then scoop out all the flesh. Remove the stones. Mash the flesh until smooth then mix thoroughly with the onion and garlic. Add the remaining ingredients and combine well. Chill for 30 minutes before serving garnished with watercress.

RAITA

½ cucumber, peeled
salt and freshly ground black pepper
150 ml/¼ pint natural yogurt, well chilled
1 tablespoon chopped mint
¼ teaspoon chilli powder
2 tablespoons chopped parsley

Coarsely grate the cucumber, then place it in a colander or sieve and sprinkle with a little salt. Leave to stand for 30 minutes, then squeeze all the liquid from the cucumber.

Beat the yogurt until smooth. Stir in the remaining ingredients, then add the cucumber, reserving a little for garnish, and mix well. Transfer to a serving dish, top with the reserved cucumber and add a little extra chilli powder. Serve within 30-60 minutes or the raita will become very watery.

Guacamole and Raita

SWEET 'N' SOUR SAUCE

2 onions, chopped
1 red pepper, deseeded and chopped
50 g/2 oz butter
2 tablespoons tomato purée
300 ml/½ pint dry cider
150 ml/¼ pint chicken stock
salt and freshly ground black pepper
few drops of Worcestershire sauce
2 tablespoons lime chutney
2 tablespoons chopped parsley
1 tablespoon arrowroot
2 tablespoons water

Sauté the onions and pepper in the butter until soft but not browned. Add all the remaining ingredients except the arrowroot and water. Bring to the boil, cover and simmer for 15-20 minutes.

Blend the arrowroot with the water and stir into the sauce. Cook for 1 minute, stirring all the time until thickened.

CUMBERLAND SAUCE

1 orange
1 lemon
225 g/8 oz redcurrant jelly
6 tablespoons red wine
25 g/1 oz soft brown sugar
salt and freshly ground black pepper
1 teaspoon arrowroot

Thinly remove the peel, without the pith, from the orange and the lemon. Shred the peel finely into matchstick lengths and place in a saucepan of fast boiling water for 3 minutes. Drain and immerse in cold water for 1 minute. Drain again and set aside.

Squeeze the juice from the fruit, strain into a saucepan with the redcurrant jelly and bring to the boil over a low heat. Stir in the wine, sugar and seasoning to taste. Blend the arrowroot with a little cold water and stir into the sauce. Bring to the boil, stirring all the time until slightly thickened. Finally stir in the blanched citrus peel.

MENU

Fish Soup

Vegetable Fondue
Garlic Mayonnaise
Guacamole
Provençal Sauce
Green Salad
French Bread

Peach Melba

Fish Soup
Make a good fish stock from fish heads and trimmings, from cheaper varieties of fish or from a stock cube. Sauté 1 finely chopped onion in a knob of butter until soft. Stir in 2 tablespoons plain flour and pour in 600 ml/1 pint fish stock. Add 450 g/1 lb skinned cod or haddock fillet, cut into small cubes, 1 bay leaf and 1 small potato, diced. Boil, then simmer for 20 minutes. Stir in 100 g/4 oz peeled cooked prawns and 100 g/4 oz shelled cooked mussels. Stir in 150 ml/¼ pint single cream and heat gently but *do not boil*. Add plenty of chopped parsley, season and serve.

Peach Melba
Use fresh or canned peach slices and good-quality vanilla ice cream. To make a melba sauce, purée 225 g/8 oz raspberries with sugar to taste, then press the fruit purée through a sieve to remove the seeds. Layer the peaches and ice cream in sundae glasses, then pour over some of the sauce and hand the rest separately.

PROVENÇAL SAUCE

1 onion
1 tablespoon oil
1 (396-g/14-oz) can tomatoes
1 clove garlic, crushed
3 tablespoons capers
1 teaspoon dried basil
1 bay leaf
sugar to taste
salt and freshly ground black pepper
1 tablespoon tomato purée

Peel and finely chop the onion. Sauté in the oil until soft but not browned. Stir in the remaining ingredients, bring to the boil, cover and simmer for 30 minutes. Remove the bay leaf, blend the sauce in a liquidiser and reheat.

HORSERADISH CREAM SAUCE

3 tablespoons grated horseradish
150 ml/¼ pint soured cream
salt and freshly ground black pepper

Stir the horseradish into the soured cream and season to taste. Chill thoroughly before serving.

Note: If grated horseradish is not available, use instead 3 tablespoons creamed horseradish sauce.

GREEN PEPPER AND GHERKIN SAUCE

1 onion, chopped
2 green peppers, deseeded and chopped
2 gherkins, sliced
25 g/1 oz butter
¼ teaspoon chilli sauce
150 ml/¼ pint chicken stock
salt and freshly ground black pepper

Sauté the onion, peppers and gherkins in the butter until golden brown. Stir in the remaining ingredients, bring to the boil and simmer for 10 minutes.

BARBECUE SAUCE

1 small onion, finely chopped
1 clove garlic, crushed
15 g/½ oz butter
250 ml/8 fl oz red wine
150 ml/¼ pint chicken stock
1 tablespoon wine vinegar
1 tablespoon brown sugar
salt and freshly ground black pepper
1 tablespoon redcurrant jelly
few drops of Tabasco sauce
2 teaspoons cornflour

Sauté the onion and garlic in the butter until soft. Add all the remaining ingredients except the cornflour. Bring to the boil, cover and simmer for 30 minutes.

Allow to cool slightly, then blend in a liquidiser or food processor until smooth. Blend the cornflour with a little of the sauce and return to the saucepan with the remaining sauce. Stirring all the time, bring the sauce to the boil and cook until thickened.

DEVILLED SAUCE

1 onion, chopped
1 green chilli, deseeded and chopped
1 green or red pepper, deseeded and chopped
25 g/1 oz butter
2 cloves garlic, crushed
2 teaspoons flour
1 tablespoon made English mustard
1 (425-g/15-oz) can chopped tomatoes
salt and freshly ground black pepper
few drops of Worcestershire sauce

Cook the onion, chilli and pepper in the butter with the garlic until well softened but not browned. Stir frequently during cooking.

Add the flour and mustard, stirring continuously, then pour in the tomatoes and bring to the boil. Stir in seasoning and Worcestershire sauce to taste, then serve hot or allow to cool and chill before serving.

Green Pepper and Gherkin Sauce

SOURED BLUE CHEESE DRESSING

*75 g/3 oz blue-vein cheese, such as
Stilton, Danish Blue or Gorgonzola
150 ml/¼ pint soured cream
few drops of lemon juice
2 tablespoons chopped chives
freshly ground black pepper*

Trim any rind off the cheese, then mash it until smooth. Gradually stir in the remaining ingredients, making sure the sauce is smooth, and chill well.

Note: If you own a liquidiser or food processor, then cut the cheese into small pieces and place it in the machine with all the remaining ingredients. Blend until smooth.

MADEIRA SAUCE

*1 onion, finely chopped
100 g/4 oz mushrooms, chopped
25 g/1 oz butter
4 tomatoes, skinned and chopped
¼ teaspoon dried basil or
1 teaspoon chopped fresh basil
3 tablespoons Madeira
150 ml/¼ pint chicken stock
salt and freshly ground black pepper
sugar to taste
fresh basil sprigs to garnish (optional)*

Sauté the onion and mushrooms in the butter until soft. Add the tomatoes and basil, cover and simmer for 5 minutes. Stir in the Madeira, stock and seasoning and cook for a further 10 minutes. Add sugar to taste and garnish with a few sprigs of fresh basil, if liked.

MAYONNAISE WITH VARIATIONS

1 egg
pinch of dry mustard
pinch of caster sugar
salt and freshly ground black pepper
300 ml/½ pint oil
1-2 tablespoons white wine vinegar
or lemon juice

Place the egg, mustard, sugar and seasoning in a liquidiser or food processor. Whisk until well blended. Continue whisking whilst adding the oil drop by drop until an emulsion is formed and the mayonnaise is thick and smooth. Finally add the wine vinegar or lemon juice.

Variations

Garlic Mayonnaise Stir a crushed clove of garlic into the finished mayonnaise.

Fresh Herb Mayonnaise Add 2 tablespoons chopped fresh herbs of your choice such as parsley, chives, tarragon or dill.

Green Mayonnaise Liquidise ½ bunch watercress in a blender or food processor and stir into the finished mayonnaise.

Thousand Island Mayonnaise To the basic mayonnaise add ½ onion, grated, 1 stick celery, finely chopped, 1 tablespoon chopped parsley, 1 tablespoon chopped capers, 1 tablespoon tomato purée and 1 tablespoon chopped green olives.

Tartare Sauce Add 3 tablespoons chopped capers, 3 tablespoons chopped gherkins and 2 tablespoons chopped parsley to the mayonnaise.

Lemon Mayonnaise To the basic mayonnaise, made using lemon juice instead of wine vinegar, add the finely grated rind of 1 lemon.

SOURED CREAM SAUCE

2 onions, chopped
3 tablespoons capers
3 tablespoons tarragon vinegar
1 teaspoon caster sugar
3 tablespoons oil
300 ml/½ pint soured cream
2 tablespoons chopped parsley

Blend the onions, capers, vinegar and sugar in a liquidiser or food processor until smooth. Transfer to a bowl and whisk in the oil, soured cream and parsley. Serve cold.

MENU

Crispy Scampi Fondue
Tartare Sauce
Barbecue Sauce
Orange Coleslaw

Iced Strawberry Mousse

Iced Strawberry Mousse
Make 150 ml/¼ pint strawberry purée from fresh or frozen strawberries. Add 2 teaspoons lemon juice and icing sugar to taste. Whisk 150 ml/¼ pint double cream until lightly whipped. Then whisk 2 egg whites until stiff. Fold the cream and egg whites into the fruit purée and pour into a rigid plastic bowl. Place in the ice-making compartment of the refrigerator or in the freezer until just firm. Spoon into dishes and serve with wafer biscuits.

Mayonnaise with a selection of ingredients to prepare the variations and Soured Cream Sauce

CHINESE SAUCE

1 small onion, chopped
1 red pepper, deseeded and chopped
2 tablespoons oil
175 ml/6 fl oz chicken stock
150 ml/¼ pint pineapple juice
1 teaspoon soy sauce
2 pieces stem ginger, finely chopped
1 (198-g/7-oz) can sweet corn, drained
1 tablespoon cornflour
2 tablespoons water

Sauté the onion and pepper in the oil until soft but not browned. Add all the remaining ingredients except the cornflour and water, cover and simmer for 10 minutes. Blend the cornflour with the water and stir into the sauce. Bring to the boil and cook for 1 minute, stirring until thickened.

SATAY SAUCE

2 onions
2 tablespoons oil
75 g/3 oz roasted peanuts
½ teaspoon chilli powder
150 ml/¼ pint warm water
15 g/½ oz soft brown sugar
salt
1-2 tablespoons soy sauce
juice of ½ lemon

Peel and slice one of the onions and fry in the oil. Chop the second onion and place in a liquidiser or food processor with the peanuts and chilli powder, blend until a paste is formed.

Add this paste to the fried onion and cook for a few minutes. Gradually stir in the water and sugar and cook for 2 minutes. Season to taste with salt, soy sauce and lemon juice and heat through.

Chinese Sauce and Satay Sauce

Salad Accompaniments

Many fondue recipes are quite rich and a fresh, crisp salad makes the ideal accompaniment for them. Even though many of the cheese-based fondues are quite filling enough to serve very simply with French bread, the contrast in texture which a crunchy salad offers is a welcome addition to the menu. If you are planning an informal fondue, served from a coffee table, it is worth remembering that guests will find it easier to eat evenly chopped salads which do not need cutting up. There are plenty of interesting ideas to choose from in this chapter, all written to complement the fondue recipes in the rest of the book.

SAUERKRAUT SALAD
SERVES 4

1 (450-g/1-lb) can sauerkraut
1 onion, chopped
4 large gherkins, chopped
2 crisp dessert apples, peeled, cored
and chopped
finely grated rind of 1 lemon
2 tablespoons chopped parsley
1 tablespoon chopped fresh basil
salt and freshly ground black pepper
sugar to taste
6 tablespoons olive oil

Drain the sauerkraut, rinse well and dry on kitchen paper. Place in a bowl and add all the remaining ingredients except the oil. Toss well together and pour over the oil. Allow to chill.

Sauerkraut Salad and Cauliflower Salad

CAULIFLOWER SALAD
SERVES 4

1 cauliflower
150 ml/¼ pint mayonnaise (page 48)
1 teaspoon wholegrain mustard
1 teaspoon paprika
pinch of sugar
salt and freshly ground black pepper
1 small lettuce, shredded
3 tomatoes, skinned and quartered
chopped parsley to garnish

Break the cauliflower into small florets and place in a saucepan of boiling salted water for 10-15 minutes. Drain and plunge into cold water then drain well on kitchen paper. Allow to cool completely.

Combine the mayonnaise, mustard, paprika, sugar and seasoning. Line a salad bowl with the shredded lettuce and pile the cauliflower and tomatoes on top. Pour over the dressing and garnish with chopped parsley.

CHINESE SALAD

SERVES 4

225 g/8 oz fresh beansprouts
1 bunch spring onions
5-cm/2-in length of cucumber
75 g/3 oz button mushrooms, sliced
3 sticks celery, thinly sliced
2 carrots, coarsely grated
1 (198-g/7-oz) can sweet corn, drained
1 tablespoon chopped parsley
1 teaspoon soy sauce
6 tablespoons vinaigrette dressing (page 58)
watercress sprigs to garnish (optional)

Wash the beansprouts thoroughly, drain well and place in a salad bowl. Trim the spring onions and chop the green ends into the beansprouts. Reserve the remaining part of the onion to garnish. Peel the cucumber, cut into matchstick lengths and stir into the bowl with the mushrooms, celery, carrot, sweetcorn and parsley.

Alternatively, the beansprouts and spring onions can be arranged in the middle of a platter and the other prepared ingredients can be neatly piled round the outside. The dressing should then be served separately, for individuals to pour over their portions as required.

Mix the soy sauce with the vinaigrette dressing and pour over the salad (if mixed). Garnish with the reserved spring onions and sprigs of watercress.

Note: To make spring onion curls, as shown in the picture, make cuts into both ends of the reserved pieces of onion. Place them in a large bowl of iced water and leave for at least 30 minutes or until the strips of onion curl up as shown.

NIÇOISE SALAD
S E R V E S   4 - 6

1 small onion, sliced
1 green pepper, deseeded and sliced
1 bunch radishes, trimmed
4 tomatoes, skinned and quartered
1 hearty lettuce, separated into wedges
1 (198-g/7-oz) can tuna fish, drained
1 (50-g/1¾-oz) can anchovies, drained
3 hard-boiled eggs, quartered
black olives
chopped parsley
vinaigrette dressing (page 58)

Place all the salad vegetables in a bowl. Arrange the tuna fish and anchovies on top. Garnish with quartered hard-boiled eggs, olives and plenty of chopped parsley. Sprinkle vinaigrette dressing over the salad just before serving.

CHILLED RATATOUILLE
S E R V E S   6

1 onion, sliced
1 clove garlic, crushed
3 tablespoons oil
1 red pepper, deseeded
1 large aubergine
450 g/1 lb courgettes
150 ml/¼ pint chicken stock
1 teaspoon sugar
1 teaspoon chopped fresh basil
salt and freshly ground black pepper
3 tomatoes, skinned and quartered

Sauté the onion and garlic in the hot oil until soft but not browned. Wash and trim the pepper, aubergine and courgettes, and cut into 2·5-cm/1-in pieces. Stir into the saucepan with the stock, sugar, basil, seasoning and tomatoes. Bring to the boil, cover and simmer for 30 minutes.

Allow to cool then chill thoroughly in the refrigerator before serving.

MENU

Avocado and Prawn Cocktail

Pork Satay Fondue
Satay Sauce
Spiced Rice Salad
Poppadums

Fresh Pineapple

Avocado and Prawn Cocktail
Mix 100 g/4 oz peeled cooked prawns with the grated rind of 1 small lemon and seasoning to taste. Stir in 2 tablespoons chopped parsley, 2 tablespoons lemon juice, 1 teaspoon tomato purée and 150 ml/¼ pint thoroughly chilled mayonnaise. Halve 2 ripe avocado pears, remove their stones, then scoop out all the flesh and reserve the shells. Roughly chop the flesh and mix with the prawns. Pile into the shells and serve garnished with whole prawns and lemon slices.

Fresh Pineapple
Select a large, ripe pineapple. Cut off the leaf and stalk ends. Peel the fruit from the top towards the base, then scoop out all the eyes. Cut the pineapple into quarters lengthways, then remove the hard core from each piece and slice the fruit. Arrange the pieces on a serving dish and sprinkle with a little Kirsch if you like. Chill lightly before serving.

AVOCADO AND MANGO SALAD

SERVES 4

2 large ripe mangos
2 large ripe avocado pears
1 fresh lime or lemon
4 tablespoons oil
1/4 teaspoon ground cinnamon

Peel the mangos, then cut the flesh off the stones in large chunks. Halve the avocado pears, remove their stones and scoop out the flesh in chunks. Reserve the shells if they are particularly large. Mix the mango and avocado in a bowl.

Pare the rind from the lime or lemon and cut it into fine strips, then add to the salad together with the juice from the fruit. Mix in the oil and cinnamon, then chill lightly before serving, spooned into the shells or in a shallow dish.

AUBERGINE SALAD

SERVES 4

675 g/1 1/2 lb aubergines
salt
1 onion, sliced
cooking oil
1 tablespoon bottled chilli sauce
1/4 teaspoon chilli powder
3 tablespoons tomato purée
salt and freshly ground black pepper
150 ml/1/4 pint chicken stock
grated Parmesan cheese to sprinkle

Trim the aubergines and cut into small cubes. Sprinkle with salt and leave for 30 minutes. Rinse well, drain and dry.

Sauté the onion and aubergine in hot oil for 2-3 minutes, then stir in the chilli sauce and chilli powder and cook for a minute. Stir in the tomato purée, seasoning and stock. Bring to the boil, cover and simmer for 10-15 minutes, until the aubergine is cooked.

Cool, then transfer the salad to a serving dish and chill well. If you like, sprinkle the salad with Parmesan cheese before serving.

PASTA SALAD
SERVES 4 - 6

225 g/8 oz wholemeal pasta shells,
bows or spirals
¼ celeriac
25 g/1 oz butter
2 red-skinned dessert apples
100 g/4 oz stuffed green olives, halved
225 g/8 oz garlic sausage, in one piece
2 hard-boiled eggs
Topping:
25 g/1 oz pine nuts or almonds
1 clove garlic
few sprigs fresh basil
4 tablespoons grated Parmesan cheese
pinch of cayenne
4 tablespoons olive oil
watercress sprigs to garnish

Cook the pasta in plenty of boiling salted water. Drain, rinse well and cool.

Peel the celeriac and cut into small cubes. Sauté in the butter for 5 minutes, until tender.

Core and slice the apples and add to the cooled pasta with the celeriac and stuffed olives. Cut the garlic sausage into cubes and stir into the pasta with the roughly chopped hard-boiled eggs.

Place the nuts, garlic, basil, cheese and cayenne in a liquidiser or food processor and grind into a paste. Gradually work in the oil until a thick consistency is formed. Spoon over the pasta salad and serve at once, garnished with sprigs of watercress.

ARTICHOKE AND BEAN VINAIGRETTE
SERVES 4

1 (425-g/15-oz) can Borlotti beans,
drained and rinsed
1 (396-g/14-oz) can artichoke hearts,
drained and halved
1 clove garlic, crushed
1 onion, sliced
2 tomatoes, skinned and chopped
salt and freshly ground black pepper
2-3 tablespoons vinaigrette dressing (page 58)

Place all the ingredients in a bowl and toss well together. Chill and serve.

MENU

Artichokes Vinaigrette

Devilled Crab Fondue
Cubes of Garlic-flavoured Bread
or Crusty Bread
Tomato Salad
Baked Potatoes

Caramelised Grapes

Artichokes Vinaigrette
Drain 2 (396-g/14-oz) cans artichoke hearts and toss in vinaigrette dressing (page 58). Chill thoroughly and garnish with plenty of freshly chopped parsley before serving.

Garlic-flavoured Bread
Make up and cook a packet of bread mix following the instructions but adding 1 large crushed clove of garlic and 2 tablespoons chopped parsley to the liquid. Shape the dough into a long loaf for ease when cutting it into cubes.

Caramelised Grapes
Wash 675 g/1½ lb seedless grapes and dry well. Take the fruit off their stalks and place in an oven-proof dish. Whisk 175 ml/6 fl oz double cream until softly whipped, and spread it evenly over the grapes. Sprinkle with enough soft brown sugar to completely cover the cream. Press down gently using the back of a spoon, then chill thoroughly in the ice-making compartment of the refrigerator or in the freezer _until thoroughly chilled_. Preheat the grill and place the grapes underneath until the sugar caramelises and cream begins to bubble. Serve immediately.

CAESAR SALAD

SERVES 4

2 slices white bread, diced
25 g/1 oz butter
1 clove garlic, crushed
150 ml/¼ pint olive oil
2 tablespoons white wine vinegar
salt and freshly ground black pepper
few drops of lemon juice
100 g/4 oz button mushrooms, sliced
4 tablespoons finely grated Parmesan cheese
1 Cos lettuce

Fry the diced bread in the butter and garlic until crisp and golden. Drain on kitchen paper.

Place the oil, vinegar, seasoning, lemon juice, mushrooms and Parmesan cheese in a screw-topped jar and shake well until an emulsion is formed.

Tear the lettuce and place in a salad bowl, pour over the dressing and toss well. Sprinkle the fried bread croûtons over the top.

GREEN SALAD

SERVES 4

1 crisp lettuce
½ cucumber, peeled and sliced
1 bunch spring onions, trimmed
2 sticks celery, sliced
1 avocado pear, peeled, sliced and tossed in lemon juice
1 bunch watercress, trimmed
chopped parsley, mint and basil
Vinaigrette Dressing:
300 ml/½ pint olive or corn oil
3 tablespoons wine vinegar
pinch each of salt, dry mustard and sugar
grated rind of ½ orange

Wash and dry all the salad vegetables. Tear the lettuce and place in a salad bowl with the prepared cucumber, spring onions, celery, avocado and watercress. Sprinkle the herbs over the top.

Blend all the ingredients for the vinaigrette dressing in a liquidiser or screw-topped jar until an emulsion is formed. Store in a screw-topped jar and shake well just before use.

Pour sufficient dressing over the green salad and toss well.

MENU

Grilled Grapefruit

Rosemary Lamb Fondue
Cumberland Sauce
Soured Cream Sauce
Caesar Salad
Chilled Ratatouille

Brandy Snaps with Cream

Grilled Grapefruit

Halve 2 grapefruit, remove the membrane and loosen the segments. Sprinkle with a little dry vermouth and brown sugar to taste. Place the fruit under a hot grill until the sugar starts to melt and caramelise. Garnish each half with a maraschino cherry and a sprig of mint.

Brandy Snaps and Cream

Melt 50 g/2 oz butter, 50 g/2 oz sugar and 65 g/2½ oz golden syrup in a saucepan. Sift 50 g/2 oz plain flour and 1 teaspoon ground ginger and stir into the melted mixture with 2 teaspoons lemon juice. Place 4 individual teaspoons of the mixture well apart (to allow for spreading) on a thoroughly greased baking tray. Bake in a moderate oven (160 C, 325 F, gas 3) for 6 to 8 minutes. Leave the brandy snaps for a minute before removing from the tray. Slide each one off carefully with a palette knife and roll them round the greased handle of a wooden spoon. When firm slide the biscuits off the spoon. Repeat with the remaining mixture.

Fill with whipped cream flavoured with a little brandy.

Caesar Salad and Green Salad

ORANGE COLESLAW
SERVES 4

350 g/12 oz white cabbage
grated rind and juice of 2 oranges
4 new carrots, scraped and coarsely grated
1 red pepper, deseeded and diced
1 small onion, finely grated
5 tablespoons mayonnaise (page 48)

Trim the outer leaves from the cabbage and shred the remainder very thinly. Place in a bowl and add the orange rind, grated carrot, diced pepper and grated onion.

Mix the orange juice with the mayonnaise and pour over the salad, tossing well.

Variations
The simple coleslaw can be varied in all sorts of ways. Combine some of the following suggestions if you like to make an elaborate salad or for substantial quantities if you are serving large numbers of guests.

Coleslaw Vinaigrette Use vinaigrette dressing (see page 58) instead of mayonnaise. Add plenty of chopped parsley to the salad.

Raisin and Walnut Coleslaw Add 50 g/2 oz raisins and 50 g/2 oz chopped walnuts to the salad.

Apple and Sultana Coleslaw Coarsely grate 2 dessert apples and mix them into the coleslaw. Add 25 g/1 oz sultanas and sprinkle with chilli powder before serving.

Pasta Slaw Add cooled, cooked pasta shapes to the above recipe. Mix in 100 g/4 oz chopped cooked ham if you like.

Caraway Seed Slaw Dress the coleslaw in a vinaigrette dressing (see page 58) instead of mayonnaise and add 2 teaspoons caraway seeds to the salad.

Herbed Coleslaw Add 2 tablespoons chopped fresh herbs to the above recipe – parsley, thyme, tarragon and chives would go well.

Orange Coleslaw and Haricot Salad

HARICOT SALAD
SERVES 4

175 g/6 oz haricot beans
3 tablespoons walnut or sesame oil
2 tablespoons tomato purée
1 tablespoon chopped parsley
1 tablespoon chopped fresh basil
1 clove garlic, crushed
salt and freshly ground black pepper
juice of ½ lemon
½ bunch spring onions, trimmed and chopped
Garnish:
50 g/2 oz walnuts, chopped
black olives
parsley sprigs

Soak the beans in plenty of cold water overnight. Drain and rinse well. Bring to the boil in fresh water and remove any scum. Reduce the heat, cover and simmer for about 30-40 minutes. Drain and allow to cool.

Heat the oil and fry the beans gently for 5-10 minutes, then stir in the tomato purée, herbs and garlic. Add sufficient water to cover the beans by about 2·5 cm/1 in. Bring to the boil and simmer uncovered for 45 minutes, or until the liquid has reduced.

Allow to cool then add the seasoning, lemon juice and spring onions. Garnish with walnuts, black olives and parsley sprigs.

RED BEAN AND BACON SALAD
SERVES 4

225 g/8 oz rindless lean bacon, chopped
1 clove garlic, crushed
1 bunch spring onions, trimmed and chopped
1 (425-g/15-oz) can red kidney beans, drained
2 tablespoons olive oil
2 tablespoons lemon juice
a few drops of Worcestershire sauce
2 tablespoons chopped parsley
salt and freshly ground black pepper
1 lettuce heart, shredded

Dry fry the bacon with the garlic until well browned. Remove from the heat and stir in all the remaining ingredients, except the lettuce, then allow to cool. Arrange the lettuce in a bowl and spoon the bean mixture on top. Serve just warm.

POTATO SALAD

S E R V E S 6

1 kg/2 lb new potatoes
3 tablespoons mayonnaise (page 48)
2 tablespoons natural yogurt
salt and freshly ground black pepper
100 g/4 oz tiny button mushrooms,
washed and dried
chopped chives or parsley to garnish

Wash the potatoes and cook in their skins in plenty of boiling salted water for about 15-20 minutes. Drain and plunge into cold water. Remove the skins and allow the potatoes to become cold. Cut into small chunks or leave whole if they are small enough.

Mix the mayonnaise with the yogurt and add the potatoes, seasoning and whole button mushrooms, tossing gently until well mixed. Garnish with chives or parsley.

Variations

Minted New Potatoes Vinaigrette Prepare the potatoes as above but omit the mushrooms. Dress with a vinaigrette dressing (see page 58) and add plenty of chopped mint. Add chopped chives or spring onions and serve with lamb fondues.

Old Potatoes These can be used quite successfully in the above recipe. Boil the potatoes in their skins, then rinse under cold water and remove the peel. Cut into chunks and continue as above.

Potato and Bacon Salad Add 100 g/4 oz crisply fried chopped bacon to the salad.

Almond and Potato Salad Lightly toast 50 g/2 oz flaked almonds and add to the salad instead of the mushrooms.

Salami and Potato Salad Prepare the salad as above, then turn it into a shallow dish. Top with plenty of shredded salami and fine onion rings.

Crunchy Potato Salad Prepare the salad as above, then top with garlic croûtons and stir them into the salad as it is served. To make garlic croûtons, cut 3 slices bread into small cubes and fry these in a mixture of butter and oil flavoured with garlic. When golden all over drain the croûtons on absorbent kitchen paper.

TOMATO SALAD

S E R V E S 4

450 g/1 lb tomatoes, skinned
1 bunch spring onions, trimmed and chopped
½ cucumber, sliced
1 bunch radishes, trimmed and sliced
1 head chicory, shredded
6-8 tablespoons vinaigrette dressing (page 58)
chopped parsley to garnish

Slice the tomatoes and arrange around the edge of a dish. Place the prepared spring onions, cucumber, radishes and chicory in a bowl and pour over the vinaigrette dressing. Toss well and pile in the centre of the dish. Sprinkle chopped parsley over the tomatoes.

Tomato Salad

Spiced Rice Salad

SPICED RICE SALAD

SERVES 4

225 g/8 oz long-grain rice
2·5-cm/1–in piece cinnamon stick
1 bay leaf
strip of pared lemon rind
1 small onion, chopped
2 tablespoons oil
pinch of turmeric
100 g/4 oz cooked peas
1 (184-g/6½-oz) can pimientos, drained and cut into strips
1 (113-g/4-oz) can smoked mussels (optional)
salt and freshly ground black pepper
6 tablespoons vinaigrette dressing (page 58)
chopped parsley to garnish

Sauté the rice, cinnamon stick, bay leaf, lemon rind and chopped onion in the hot oil, stirring all the time for 2-3 minutes. Add the turmeric and plenty of boiling water and cook the rice until tender. Drain, removing the cinnamon stick, bay leaf and lemon rind. Rinse the rice in cold water.

When cold add the peas, pimientos, mussels and seasoning. Pour over the vinaigrette dressing and toss well. Sprinkle with chopped parsley.

BROWN RICE AND WALNUT SALAD

SERVES 4

225 g/8 oz brown rice
2·5-cm/1–in piece cinnamon stick
1 bay leaf
strip of pared lemon rind
1 small onion, chopped
100 g/4 oz chopped walnuts
1 bunch spring onions, trimmed and chopped
6 tablespoons vinaigrette dressing (page 58)

Prepare the rice as for Spiced Rice Salad. Drain and rinse, then mix with the walnuts and spring onions while still warm. Pour the dressing over the rice and toss well, then leave to marinate for at least 30 minutes before serving.

Dessert Fondues

If you favour the sweet course of the meal then you will delight in the idea of serving a pot of luscious chocolate fondue, dark cherry fondue or creamy mallow fondue. Each of the recipes in this chapter offers serving suggestions but it is worth planning the menu carefully if you intend making a sweet fondue. Keep the starter, if any, light and the main course simple so that everyone will have room for the ample dessert to follow.

DARK FUDGE FONDUE

SERVES 2

25 g/1 oz butter
75 g/3 oz dark soft brown sugar
175 ml/6 fl oz milk
1 tablespoon black treacle
1 tablespoon cornflour
2 tablespoons water

Place the butter and sugar in a saucepan and heat gently until the sugar has dissolved, stirring all the time. Bring to the boil and simmer for 1 minute, still stirring. Stir in the milk and treacle. Blend the cornflour with the water and pour in. Bring to the boil, stirring continuously, and simmer for 2-3 minutes.

Pour into a fondue pan and serve hot.

Serving Suggestion
Serve with sponge fingers, plain biscuits and pieces of banana dipped in lemon juice.

APRICOT CHEESE FONDUE

SERVES 4

1 (411-g/14½-oz) can apricot halves
1 tablespoon cornflour
1 (85-g/3-oz) packet cream cheese
150 ml/¼ pint double cream
1 tablespoon lemon curd
2 tablespoons apricot brandy

Drain the apricot halves and blend the fruit in a liquidiser to make a purée. Mix a little of the apricot juice with the cornflour. Pour the remainder into a fondue pan with the purée and heat gently. Add the cornflour and cook until the fondue begins to thicken.

Divide the cream cheese into small pieces and stir into the fondue until melted. Gradually add the remaining ingredients and reheat, stirring continuously. *Do not allow to boil.*

Serving Suggestion
Serve with cubes of gingerbread or sponge fingers to dip into the fondue.

Apricot Cheese Fondue

BLACK FOREST FONDUE

S E R V E S   4

1 (390-g/13¾-oz) can black cherry pie filling
1 (425-g/15-oz) can stoned black cherries,
drained
150 ml/¼ pint double cream
1 tablespoon Kirsch liqueur
few drops of Maraschino essence

Place the pie filling and black cherries in a fondue pan and heat gently. Stir in the cream, Kirsch and Maraschino essence and reheat, taking care *not to boil*.

Serving Suggestion

Serve with cubes of chocolate cake, small almond macaroons and meringue fingers.

Note: To make meringue fingers, take 2 egg whites and 100 g/4 oz caster sugar. Whisk the egg whites until they stand in stiff peaks. Still whisking continuously with an electric mixer, gradually add the sugar and whisk until the meringue is very stiff and glossy. Fit a piping bag with a large plain nozzle and line two baking trays with non-stick baking parchment. Pipe neat fingers of meringue on to the trays and dry out in a very cool oven (110C, 200F, gas ¼) for 3-4 hours.

CHOCOLATE MINT FONDUE

SERVES 6

450 g/1 lb plain chocolate, grated
2 tablespoons Royal Mint Chocolate liqueur
150 ml/¼ pint double cream

Place the chocolate in a fondue pan and allow to melt over a low heat. Stir in the liqueur and cream and re-heat gently, stirring continuously. *Do not allow to boil.*

Serving Suggestion

Serve with chocolate mints or plain mints and slices of banana dipped in icing sugar.

BLACKCURRANT CREAM FONDUE

SERVES 4

225 g/8 oz blackcurrants, trimmed
100 g/4 oz sugar
25 g/1 oz butter
175 ml/6 fl oz plus 1 tablespoon water
150 ml/¼ pint double cream

Place the blackcurrants, sugar, butter and 175 ml/6 fl oz water in a saucepan and allow the sugar to dissolve over a low heat. Bring to the boil and simmer until the blackcurrants are soft. Allow to cool slightly then sieve the fruit.

Blend the cornflour with the 1 tablespoon of water. Pour the fruit purée into a fondue pan and stir in the cornflour mixture. Bring to the boil, stirring and simmer for 2 minutes. Add the cream. Reheat gently, stirring all the time, but *do not allow to boil.*

Serving Suggestion

Serve Langue de Chat biscuits to dip into the fondue.

MENU

Gingered Melon Cup
Lemon Grilled Plaice
New Potatoes
Sautéed Courgettes

Chocolate Mint Fondue

Gingered Melon Cup

Halve 1 small honeydew melon. Discard the seeds, then cut the flesh into cubes or scoop it out with a melon baller. Divide between four individual dishes and top each with 2 tablespoons ginger wine. Chill thoroughly before serving.

Lemon Grilled Plaice

Allow 2 plaice fillets per person. Sprinkle each piece of fish with a little grated lemon rind and lemon juice. Season the fish and lay the fillets on a grill rack. Dot with butter and grill for about 10 minutes, until cooked and lightly browned. Sprinkle with chopped fresh tarragon or parsley and serve at once.

Sautéed Courgettes

Wash, trim and thinly slice small young courgettes. Toss them quickly, over a high heat, in butter and sprinkle with seasoning to taste. Add plenty of chopped parsley and sprinkle a little grated Parmesan cheese over just before they are served.

Blackcurrant Cream Fondue

RASPBERRY MALLOW FONDUE

SERVES 4

225 g/8 oz raspberries, fresh or frozen
1 (175-g/6-oz) packet marshmallows
150 ml/¼ pint double cream
few drops of lemon juice

Defrost raspberries if frozen. Blend in a liquidiser into a purée. Place the raspberry purée, marshmallows and cream in a fondue pan and allow to melt over a low heat, stirring all the time. Add the lemon juice and reheat, but *do not allow to boil*.

Serving Suggestion

This type of fondue is particularly popular with children. Serve with wafer biscuits and macaroons.

MOCHA FONDUE

SERVES 4

225 g/8 oz plain chocolate
1 tablespoon instant coffee granules
175 ml/6 fl oz double cream
1 tablespoon sherry

Grate the chocolate and mix with the coffee granules. Place the cream in a fondue pan and add the chocolate and coffee. Heat gently, stirring continuously until the fondue is thoroughly blended and smooth. Stir in the sherry and heat gently, then transfer to a fondue burner to serve.

Serving Suggestion

Serve cubes of plain sponge cake, sponge fingers or marshmallows to dip into the fondue.

MENU

Grilled Lamb Chops with Rosemary and Garlic
Artichoke and Bean Vinaigrette
Potato Salad
Garlic Bread

Raspberry Mallow Fondue

Grilled Lamb Chops with Rosemary and Garlic

Trim any surplus fat from 8 best end of neck lamb cutlets. Sprinkle with chopped fresh rosemary, crushed cloves of garlic to taste and a little seasoning. Place under a very hot preheated grill and turn over quickly to seal both sides. Grill for 8 to 10 minutes, turning frequently, until cooked to your liking. Garnish with sprigs of watercress and grilled halved tomatoes.

Garlic Bread

Cream 100 g/4 oz butter with 2 crushed cloves of garlic and a little seasoning. Cut a French loaf into slices, leaving them all slightly attached underneath, then spread with the garlic butter. Press the slices back together, wrap in cooking foil and bake in a moderately hot oven (200 C, 400 F, gas 6) for 15 minutes.

Mocha Fondue

SPICED CHOCOLATE FONDUE

SERVES 4

225 g/8 oz plain chocolate
6 tablespoons double cream
¼ teaspoon ground nutmeg
¼ teaspoon cinnamon
grated rind of ½ orange

Grate the chocolate and place in a fondue pan. Gradually stir in the cream and spices and heat gently, stirring all the time. *Do not allow to boil.* Just before serving stir in the orange rind.

Serving Suggestion

Macaroons and sponge fingers are good accompaniments to this fondue or you can serve pieces of fresh fruit and dessert biscuits as shown below.

Spiced Chocolate Fondue

CHOCOLATE BANANA FONDUE

SERVES 4

225 g/8 oz plain chocolate
2 tablespoons golden syrup
2 tablespoon rum
2 large bananas
150 ml/¼ pint double cream

Cut the chocolate into small pieces and melt it in a fondue pan with the syrup and rum.

Meanwhile, thoroughly mash the bananas and stir in the cream. Alternatively purée the fruit in a liquidiser. Stir this banana cream into the fondue and heat very gently. *Do not allow to boil.*

Serving Suggestion

Serve cubes of plain cake, small almond macaroons and semi-sweet finger biscuits with the fondue.

BRANDIED ORANGE FONDUE
SERVES 4

225 g/8 oz plain chocolate
150 ml/¼ pint fresh orange juice
1 tablespoon arrowroot
1 teaspoon finely grated orange rind
2 tablespoons brandy

Melt the chocolate in a fondue pan over a low heat. Blend the orange juice with the arrowroot and stir into the melted chocolate until the fondue thickens. Add the grated orange rind and brandy and serve immediately.

Serving Suggestion
Make some small choux pastry profiteroles and fill with a little whipped cream. These are delicious dipped into the fondue and this would make an ideal dessert for a dinner party.

RHUBARB AND GINGER FONDUE
SERVES 4

1 (539-g/1 lb 3-oz) can rhubarb
1 tablespoon arrowroot
175 ml/6 fl oz double cream
pinch of ground ginger
sugar to taste

Drain the rhubarb and blend the fruit in a liquidiser to make a purée. Mix the rhubarb juice with the arrowroot and pour into a fondue pan with the purée. Heat gently, stirring all the time until thickened. Stir in the cream, ginger and sugar, if required. Reheat but *do not allow to boil.*

Serving Suggestion
Serve brandy snaps or cubes of gingerbread with this fondue.

MENU

Herb Dip

Garlic Prawns
Potato and Bacon Salad
Simple Cucumber Salad

Rhubarb and Ginger Fondue

Herb Dip
Beat 4 tablespoons finely chopped fresh herbs into 100 g/4 oz cream cheese. Stir in 1 teaspoon English mustard, seasoning and enough natural yogurt to make a soft dip. Add a dash of Worcestershire sauce and serve with sticks of celery or carrot, cauliflower florets, crisps or crackers.

Garlic Prawns
Finely chop and fry 1 small onion in 25 g/1 oz butter with 1 large crushed clove of garlic. When soft, add 450 g/1 lb peeled cooked prawns (defrosted if frozen) and cook gently until hot. Stir in 2 tablespoons chopped parsley and the grated rind of 1 lemon. Serve hot with Granary bread.

Simple cucumber salad
Trim and thinly slice 1 small cucumber. Arrange on a platter and sprinkle with chopped chives, a little vinegar and olive oil. Chill lightly before serving.

Note: If you plan to serve a substantial meal, then you can make two fondues as part of one menu, but make sure that you have suitable pans to hand. For example, you could serve a Neuchâtel Fondue (see page 19) as the main course in this menu. The cheese fondue can be prepared in an earthenware fondue pot. If you have an attractive flameproof casserole or saucepan, then you may like to make the sweet fondue in that.

Drinks to Serve with Fondues

SPICED CIDER CUP
SERVES 6 - 8

1 orange
6 cloves
1 cinnamon stick
150 ml/¼ pint medium sherry
1·25 litres/2½ pints dry cider

Wash the orange then stick it with the cloves. Place the orange in a saucepan with the cinnamon stick and the sherry. Pour in the cider and heat gently without allowing the drink to become very hot or to boil. The slower the heating process, the better the drink.

Ladle the cider into heatproof glasses and serve very warm. Keep the remainder hot over a plate warmer or on top of the cooker.

MULLED WINE
SERVES 6

1 large orange
6 cloves
1 cinnamon stick
150 ml/¼ pint brandy or rum
2 tablespoons demerara sugar
1 bottle inexpensive full-bodied red wine

Wash the orange, then stick it with the cloves. Place in a saucepan and add the cinnamon stick. Pour in the brandy or rum, stir in the sugar and add the wine. Heat very gently (best over the lowest setting available) until the wine is just hot; do not overheat or boil.

Ladle the mulled wine into heatproof glasses and keep the remainder warm over a plate warmer.

CIDER PUNCH
SERVES 6 - 8

1 orange
2 tablespoons brandy
1·25 litres/2½ pints dry cider
2 dessert apples
900 ml/1½ pints soda water

Cut the ends off the orange, then thinly slice it and place it in a punch bowl or jug with the brandy. Pour in the cider and chill for several hours.

Before serving the punch, core and thinly slice the apples, add them to the cider and pour in the soda water. Add plenty of ice and serve in long glasses.

SANGRIA

SERVES 8-10

1 bottle red wine
1 large bottle lemonade
1 lemon
1 orange
1 apple
2 tablespoons caster sugar

Thoroughly chill the wine and lemonade before serving. It is best to do this overnight if possible.

Wash the fruit, then thinly slice the lemon and orange, and core and thinly slice the apple. Place the fruit in a large bowl or jug with the sugar, then pour in the wine and lemonade. Stir well and serve immediately.

CUCUMBER COOLER

SERVES 6-8

¼ cucumber
100 g/4 oz firm strawberries
1 bottle dry white wine
a few sprigs of lemon balm,
lemon verbena or mint
1 large bottle tonic water
6 tablespoons brandy (optional)

Trim the end off the cucumber and if the skin is coarse, then peel it very lightly indeed – the vegetable should still be dark green even when it is peeled. Slice the cucumber very thinly and put the slices in a large bowl or jug.

Hull and slice the strawberries, add them to the cucumber with the herbs and pour in the wine. Chill for 3-4 hours before serving. Just before serving, add the tonic water and brandy, stir, then ladle into glasses.

WHITE WINE AND SODA

SERVES 6

1 lemon
1 bottle dry white wine
few sprigs of mint
soda water

Wash the lemon, cut off the ends, then thinly slice the fruit and place it in a jug. Pour the wine over and add the mint, then chill for 3-4 hours.

Take large glasses and put several ice cubes in each. Pour in the wine, adding some lemon slices and a sprig of mint to each. Top up with soda water and serve at once. This is very refreshing for hot summer days.

Index

Green mayonnaise 48
Green pepper and gherkin sauce 46
Green salad 58
Gruyère fondue with walnuts 21
Guacamole 43
Guacamole fondue 14

Ham and horseradish fondue 16
Haricot salad 61
Herb bread, hot 30
Herb dip 73
Herb (fresh) mayonnaise 48
Herbed coleslaw 61
Horseradish cream sauce 45

Ice cream and chocolate sauce 30

Lamb:
   Grilled lamb chops with rosemary
      and garlic 70
   Marsala lamb fondue 37
   Rosemary lamb fondue 37
Leeks vinaigrette 22
Lemon grilled plaice 69
Lemon mayonnaise 48
Lobster fondue 18
Lymeswold fondue 31

Madeira sauce 47
Marsala lamb fondue 37
Mayonnaise and variations 48
Meatball fondues 38
Melon:
   Gingered melon cup 69
   Melon and grapefruit cocktail 35
Meringue fingers 66
Meringues and strawberries 27
Minted new potatoes vinaigrette 62
Mocha fondue 70
Mulled wine 74
Mushroom and mustard fondue 26
Mustards 26

Neuchâtel fondue 19
Niçoise salad 55

Onion and caraway fondue 21
Orange:
   Brandied orange fondue 73
   Marinated pork in orange fondue 39
   Orange coleslaw 61
   Oranges in caramel sauce 19
Oriental fondue 38

Pasta coleslaw 61

Pasta salad 57
Peach melba 44
Peanut meatballs 38
Pineapple:
   Cheese and pineapple fondue 27
   Fresh pineapple 55
Plaice:
   Lemon grilled plaice 69
Pork:
   Marinated pork in orange fondue 39
   Pork satay fondue 37
Potato:
   Potato salads 62
   Sautéed garlic potatoes 35
   Swiss rosti 14
Prawn. *See also* Scampi
   Avocado and prawn cocktail 55
   Garlic prawns 73
Provençal sauce 45

Raisin and walnut coleslaw 61
Raita 43
Raspberry mallow fondue 70
Ratatouille, chilled 55
Red bean and bacon salad 61
Rhubarb and ginger fondue 73
Rice:
   Brown rice and walnut salad 63
   Spiced rice salad 63
Rosemary lamb fondue 37

Sage fondue 31
Salads:
   Artichoke and bean vinaigrette 57
   Aubergine salad 56
   Avocado and mango salad 56
   Brown rice and walnut salad 63
   Caesar salad 58
   Cauliflower salad 53
   Chilled ratatouille 55
   Chinese salad 54
   Coleslaws 61
   Green salad 58
   Haricot salad 61
   Niçoise salad 55
   Pasta salad 57
   Potato salads 62
   Red bean and bacon salad 61
   Sauerkraut salad 53
   Simple cucumber salad 73
   Spiced rice salad 63
   Tomato salad 62
Salami and potato salad 62
Sangria 75
Satay sauce 50
Sauces:
   Barbecue sauce 46
   Chinese sauce 50
   Cumberland sauce 44
   Devilled sauce 46

Green pepper and gherkin sauce 46
Horseradish cream sauce 45
Madeira sauce 47
Mayonnaise and variations 48
Provençal sauce 45
Satay sauce 50
Soured blue cheese dressing 47
Soured cream sauce 48
Sweet 'n' sour sauce 44
Sauerkraut salad 53
Scampi:
   Crispy scampi fondue 36
Seafood fondue 16
Smoked haddock fondue 36
Smoked mackerel pâté 19
Smoky bacon fondue 30
Sorrel fondue 15
Soup:
   Fish soup 44
   Fresh tomato soup with basil 27
Soured blue cheese dressing 47
Soured cream sauce 48
Spiced chocolate fondue 72
Spiced cider cup 74
Spiced rice salad 63
Spring onion curls 54
Stilton fondue 23
Strawberry mousse 48
Sweet corn and pepper fondue 28
Sweet 'n' sour sauce 44
Swiss rosti 14

Tartare sauce 48
Thousand island mayonnaise 48
Three-cheese fondue 24
Tomato:
   To skin tomatoes 21
   Fresh tomato soup with basil 27
   Tomato salad 62
Tuna and fresh tomato fondue 21

Vegetable fondue 34

Walnut:
   Brown rice and walnut salad 63
   Gruyère fondue with walnuts 21
   Raisin and walnut coleslaw 61
White wine and soda 75